Why do dolphins squeak?

First published as Why Why Why in 2008 by
Miles Kelly Publishing Ltd, Bardfield Centre,
Great Bardfield, Essex, CM7 4SL

Copyright © Miles Kelly Publishing Ltd 2008

This edition published 2009

2 4 6 8 10 9 7 5 3 1

Editorial Director Belinda Gallagher
Art Director Jo Brewer
Editorial Assistant Carly Blake
Volume Designer Sally Lace
Cover Designer Jo Brewer
Indexer Hilary Bird
Production Manager Elizabeth Brunwin
Reprographics Anthony Cambray, Ian Paulyn
Editions Manager Bethan Ellish
Character Cartoonist Mike Foster

All artwork from the Miles Kelly Archives

ISBN 978-1-84810-169-2

Printed in China

British Library Cataloguing-in-Publication Data
A catalogue record for this book is available
from the British Library

Made with paper from a sustainable forest

www.mileskelly.net
info@mileskelly.net

Contents

What is the biggest whale? 4

How heavy is a whale? 5

Can whales breathe under water? 5

What is a dolphin? 6

Can dolphins smell? 7

What is a porpoise? 7

Why do whales splash backwards? 8

Which dolphin is almost blind? 9

Why do barnacles stick to whales? 9

Do dolphins live in schools? 10

Why are dolphins so clever? 11

Why do dolphins squeak? 11

Why do whales puff and blow? 12

Which whale dives the deepest? 13

What do whales like to eat? 13

Are whales and dolphins
   like people? 14

How do whales and dolphins
   keep warm? 15

When did whales walk on land? 15

How do dolphins catch fish? 16

Which whale eats giant squid? 17

What is a group of whales called? 17

Do all whales have teeth? 18

Why do whales sieve the sea? 19

Do whales make curtains? 19

Which whale can surf? 20

Why do dolphins swim near boats? 21

Can dolphins perform tricks? 21

Which whales swordfight? 22

Why do whales sing? 23

Do whales go on holiday? 23

How big is a baby whale? 24

Do whales and dolphins drink milk? 24

Which baby whale changes colour? 25

Why do dolphins leap? 26

How do dolphins say hello? 27

Do people go whale watching? 27

Do people still hunt whales? 28

Why do whales and dolphins get
   stranded? 29

Who was swallowed by a whale? 29

Quiz time 30

Index 32

What is the biggest whale?

The blue whale is the biggest whale. In fact it is the biggest animal ever to have lived. Some grow up to 30 metres long – the same as 18 people swimming end-to-end. Like all whales, the blue whale spends its entire life in water.

Remember

How long can a bottlenose whale hold its breath? Read these pages again if you can't remember.

Every year, grey whales swim 20,000 kilometres in less than six weeks. A good human swimmer would take 30 weeks to swim the same distance.

How heavy is a whale?

Very heavy! Some whales, such as killer whales and minke whales, reach up to 10 tonnes in weight. This isn't as heavy as the blue whale, which weighs a massive 150 tonnes – that's the weight of 35 elephants!

Blue whale

Can whales breathe under water?

No, they can't. Whales breathe air through a blowhole on the top of their head. They have to hold their breath when they dive underwater to feed, then come back to the surface for air. The bottlenose whale can hold its breath for more than one hour!

What is a dolphin?

A dolphin is a mammal that lives in the sea and some rivers. They come to the surface to breathe air. Dolphins are excellent swimmers and can often be seen leaping above the waves. There are about 35 types of dolphin and most grow to 3 metres in length.

Bottlenose dolphins

Faster, faster!

The fin whale can swim at 20 kilometres an hour, making it one of the fastest whales. It is also the second largest whale, reaching 26 metres in length!

Can dolphins smell?

Dolphins have little or no sense of smell. They use taste to tell them about the foods they eat. They can taste the water too, to see if there might be any other bits of food drifting nearby!

Draw

On a piece of paper, draw a dolphin outline and colour it in any pattern you wish. Give your dolphin a name.

What is a porpoise?

Porpoises are mammals that look similar to dolphins. However, porpoises are smaller and grow to around 2 metres or less. There are six types of porpoise, which all live in the sea. Porpoises have spade-shaped teeth, unlike dolphins, which have cone-shaped teeth.

Spectacled porpoise

Why do whales splash backwards?

Whales jump out of the sea and crash down backwards as a way of sending messages to other whales. This is called breaching. They may also splash backwards to get rid of barnacles that stick to their skin. Even humpback whales can breach – and they weigh 30 tonnes!

Breaching
humpback whale

Think

Barnacles are a type of shellfish. Can you think of any other creatures that live in shells?

Which dolphin is almost blind?

The Indus River dolphin lives in rivers in India. It has tiny eyes and is almost blind because the water is so muddy. To find its way in the water, it drags its flipper along the riverbed.

Indus River dolphin

Why do barnacles stick to whales?

Barnacles are a type of shellfish that stick to moving whales. They can catch more of their favourite food – tiny shrimps and plants called plankton – when they are on the move.

Biggest brain!

The sperm whale has the biggest brain in the world! It weighs 8 kilograms and is five times bigger than a human brain. However, the sperm whale is not the cleverest animal.

Do dolphins live in schools?

Many kinds of dolphin live in groups called schools. Bottlenose dolphins live in small groups of two to four animals, but common dolphins live in bigger groups, sometimes of over 2000. Occasionally, many kinds of dolphin join together to form even bigger groups of many thousands.

Swim

When you go swimming see if you can move like a dolphin. Keep your legs together and wave them up and down.

Why are dolphins so clever?

Dolphins have large brains, which means they are clever, intelligent animals. They can learn tricks such as leaping through hoops and knocking balls with their noses. They can even solve simple puzzles and count!

Why do dolphins squeak?

Dolphins use squeaking sounds to talk to each other and to surprise their prey. The sounds bounce off nearby objects and by listening to the echoes that bounce back, the dolphins can work out where things are.

Common dolphins

Rescue me!

There are stories of dolphins saving people in danger in the sea. The dolphins might nudge them to shore, and some stories even tell of dolphins protecting people from sharks!

Why do whales puff and blow?

Whales puff and blow when they breathe. Whales, dolphins and porpoises breathe through a blowhole on top of their head, instead of through a nose. When a whale surfaces, it pushes old air, and a slimy liquid called mucus, out through its blowhole. This is called a 'blow'.

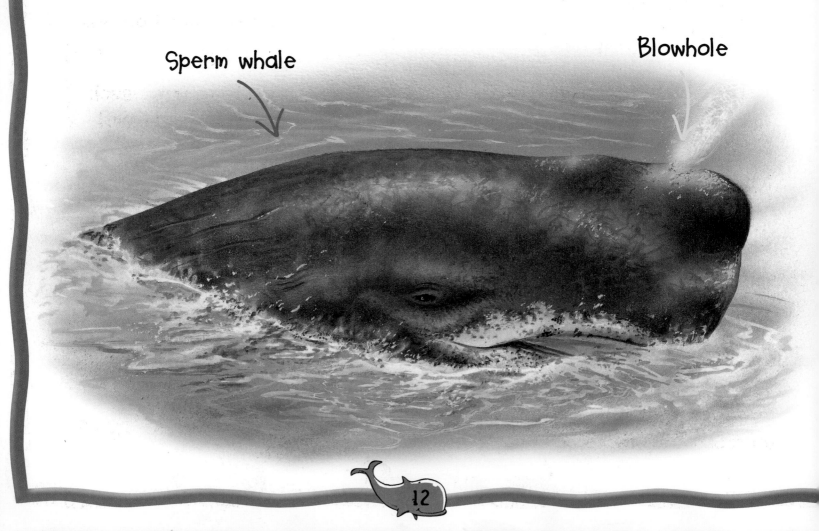

Sperm whale

Blowhole

Sperm whale diving

It's a bit blowy!

All whales have 'blows' of different shapes and sizes. The sperm whale's blow is unusual – it is less than 2 metres in height, quite bushy, and angled forwards to the left.

Which whale dives the deepest?

The sperm whale does. Before diving, the sperm whale comes to the surface to take some deep breaths. Then it arches its back so that its body points straight down. This helps it to plunge quickly into the depths – down to 3000 metres!

Blow

With a straw, suck up some water but don't swallow it! Aim the straw up and blow the water out like a whale.

What do whales like to eat?

All whales are carnivores, which means that they eat other animals. There are two types of whale – baleen and toothed. Baleen whales eat tiny shrimps called krill. Toothed whales eat mainly fish, and some even crunch up crabs and shellfish!

Are whales and dolphins like people?

Whales, dolphins and porpoises are mammals, just like people. They are warm-blooded like us and have the same parts inside their bodies, too. They have a skeleton of bones, a stomach, a heart to pump blood and lungs to breathe air.

Inside a dolphin

Whale-size feast!

In summer, blue whales can eat 4 tonnes of food a day. That's 1.5 million calories – the same as eating 7350 hamburgers. That's why blue whales are so heavy.

How do whales and dolphins keep warm?

Unlike many mammals, whales and dolphins don't have a thick coat of fur to keep them warm. Instead, they have a thick layer of fat called blubber just under the skin. In large whales the blubber can be more than 50 centimetres thick!

When did whales walk on land?

About 50 million years ago, whales lived on land. They used their flippers as legs, but slowly over time they lived more in water. The earliest whale was *Pakicetus*, which grew to about 2 metres long. *Pakicetus* could run on land and swim.

Name

Have a look at the big picture. Can you name any of the body parts inside the dolphin?

Pakicetus

How do dolphins catch fish?

Dolphins use their speedy swimming to catch fish. They twist and turn through the water and snap at their prey. Bottlenose dolphins work together to gather a shoal of fish into a tight group called a 'bait-ball'. The dolphins dash into the bait-ball and try to grab the fish.

Paint

The sperm whale's favourite food is giant squid. Think about your favourite foods and paint a delicious picture of them.

Which whale eats giant squid?

The sperm whale only eats giant squid, which live in very deep water. To hunt for its favourite food, the sperm whale can hold its breath for more than two hours. The largest giant squid ever caught by a sperm whale was 12 metres long!

Sperm whale

Bait-ball

Melon head!

Dolphins and toothed whales have a 'melon' – a large, fluid-filled lump at the front of their head. It helps the animals' squeaks go in the right direction when they are hunting.

What is a group of whales called?

A group of whales is called a pod. Normally there are 20 to 30 whales in a pod. The older females are usually in charge. They decide when to rest, when to hunt and where to travel during the year.

Do all whales have teeth?

Pilot whale

Only 'toothed whales', such as sperm whales and pilot whales, have teeth. They are active hunters and feed on squid, fish and other mammals that live in the sea. Some toothed whales only have two teeth. These whales have to suck in their prey and swallow it whole.

Play
Mix some sand with a few marbles. With a friend, see who can sieve the most sand and find the marbles!

Why do whales sieve the sea?

Some whales, such as the humpback whale, sieve the sea for their food of tiny sea creatures called krill. These whales have lots of long, bendy strips called baleen that hang in their mouth. The whale pushes water out through its baleen, which catches food like a giant filter.

Humpback whale →

Big ears!

Hector's dolphin is sometimes called the Mickey Mouse dolphin, because its back fin is shaped like the cartoon character's ears!

Do whales make curtains?

The humpback whale makes 'bubble-curtains'. It dives down, then swims up slowly in small circles, breathing out as it moves. This creates a curtain of rising bubbles, which keeps krill and other food close together – ready for a big mouthful!

Which whale can surf?

The killer whale can. Killer whales, or orcas, will surf onto a beach by swimming quickly towards the shore, to grab a young seal or sea lion. Then the whale wriggles back into the sea, holding its victim in its sharp, back-curved teeth.

Killer whale

Why do dolphins swim near boats?

Lots of dolphins like to swim in the big waves created by moving boats. This is called bow-riding. People aren't sure why dolphins do this. They may be waiting for leftover food to be thrown overboard, or saving energy by surfing on the ship's wave.

↑ Pacific white-sided dolphin

It's my name!

Humpback whales get their name because of the way they hump their back up out of the water before they dive down into the ocean to feed.

Have a go

What trick can you do? Try patting your head and rubbing your tummy at the same time.

Can dolphins perform tricks?

Yes they can. Many people visit sea-life centres and aquariums to see dolphins performing in shows. When the dolphins are being trained they have been known to change the tricks and invent new puzzles to make them more fun.

Which whales swordfight?

Narwhals do. Only male narwhals have a tusk. They use it to show off and fight with other males during the breeding season, to win over a female. The tusk is actually a very long, sharp tooth that grows in a corkscrew pattern. It can grow up to 3 metres long.

Narwhals fighting

Long in the tusk!

In the 16th century, Queen Elizabeth I received a carved tusk worth £10,000 – the cost of a castle. It was believed to be a unicorn horn, but was actually a narwhal tusk!

Singing humpback whale

Why do whales sing?

Whales 'sing' when they want to find a partner. The male humpback whale sings while hanging in the water with its flippers and tail dangling down. It makes wails, squeaks and shrieks in a pattern that it repeats. This sometimes lasts for up to 22 hours!

Play

Pretend to be a narwhal! Attach a straw to your nose with a piece of blu-tac, as your tusk!

Do whales go on holiday?

Yes, they do, in a way! Whales, dolphins and porpoises go on long journeys at the same time each year – this is called migration. They travel to find the best food. Some whales travel to warmer, calmer waters to give birth.

How big is a baby whale?

Grey whale and calf

Very big! A newborn grey whale, called a calf, is about 5 metres long and weighs half a tonne. It grows inside its mother for 13 months before it is born. The blue whale calf is the biggest animal baby – it is 7 metres long and weighs 3 tonnes at birth!

Do whales and dolphins drink milk?

Yes they do, just like all other mammals. Most feed on their mother's milk for about a year. The milk is rich and full of goodness. The blue whale calf drinks 350 litres of milk a day – enough to fill four bathtubs!

Dolphin-zilla!

Killer whales are not actually whales, but the biggest members of the dolphin family. Males grow up to 9 metres and weigh 10 tonnes.

Beluga whale
and calf

Discover

Were you a big baby or a little one? Look back at old photos of yourself to find out.

Which baby whale changes colour?

Adult beluga whales are completely white. Babies are dark or pinky-grey at birth. It takes about five years for them to turn completely white. The beluga calf grows inside its mother for 15 months. Once born, it swims to the surface to take its first breath.

Why do dolphins leap?

Dolphins leap for several reasons. On long journeys, leaping can save energy – it is much easier to move through air than through water. They might also leap to see fish from above the water, or simply for fun. The dusky dolphin is one of the most impressive leapers!

Dusky dolphin

How do dolphins say hello?

Dolphins rub, stroke and roll over each other to say "hello". Whales, dolphins and porpoises have very sensitive skin. Touching and stroking happens more during breeding time. A mother whale often strokes her baby to give it comfort and warmth.

Atlantic spotted dolphins

Touch

Dolphins have very sensitive skin. Did you know that your fingertips, feet and lips are some of the most sensitive parts of your body?

Do people go whale watching?

When people are on holiday they may go on boat trips to see whales in their natural surroundings, and scientists watch whales to learn about how they live. Sometimes, whales are frightened or disturbed by this, so it's important to explore their behaviour with care.

Sea-sleeping!

Dolphins sleep with just one half of their brain at a time, and with one eye open. Dolphins need to stay half awake to come to the surface to breathe.

Do people still hunt whales?

People have hunted whales for thousands of years. Today, some hunting continues, but many whales are now protected. These animals were valuable because their blubber could be burned in lamps, their meat could be eaten and their baleen strips were used for clothing and tools.

Smile!

The bowhead whale has a big mouth. In fact, it has the biggest mouth of any animal. It measures 10 metres around the lips and 20 people could fit inside it!

Whale hunting in the 19th century

Why do whales and dolphins get stranded?

No one knows why whales and dolphins get stranded, or washed up and stuck on the shore. The animals may have been disturbed by storms, become ill or simply got lost.

Who was swallowed by a whale?

In the Bible, a man called Jonah was swallowed by a whale and he lived inside it for three days and three nights. Jonah prayed to God that he would get out of the whale. Eventually, the whale spat Jonah out onto dry land.

Jonah and the whale

Think

There are many different types of whale. Can you name three different whales in this book?

29

Quiz time

Do you remember what you have read about whales and dolphins? These questions will test your memory. The pictures will help you. If you get stuck, read the pages again.

page 9

3. Which dolphin is almost blind?

page 10

4. Do dophins live in schools?

page 4

1. What is the biggest whale?

page 13

5. What do whales like to eat?

page 7

2. Can dolpins smell?

page 14

6. Are whales and dolphins like people?

7. What is a group of whales called?

page 17

11. Which baby whale changes colour?

page 25

8. Do all whales have teeth?

page 18

12. How do dolphins say hello?

page 27

13. Why do whales and dolphins get stranded?

page 29

9. Which whale can surf?

page 20

10. Do whales and dolphins drink milk?

page 24

Answers

1. The blue whale
2. No, not very well
3. The Indus River dolphin
4. Yes, they do
5. Fish, crabs and krill
6. Yes, they are mammals like people
7. A pod
8. Only toothed whales have teeth
9. The killer whale
10. Yes, they do
11. A baby beluga whale
12. They rub, stroke and roll over each other
13. Because they get lost or ill

Index

A
aquariums 21
Atlantic spotted
   dolphin 27

B
baby whales 24–25, 27
'bait-ball' 16–17
baleen whales 13, 19,
   28
barnacles 8, 9
beluga whale 25
Bible 29
blind dolphins 9
blood 14
blowholes 5, 12
'blows' 12, 13
blubber 15, 28
blue whale 4–5, 14, 24
bones 14
bottlenose dolphin 6–7,
   10, 16
bottlenose whale 5
bow-riding 21
bowhead whale 28
brains 9, 11, 27
breaching 8
breath-holding 5, 17
breathing 5, 12, 14, 27
breeding 22, 27
'bubble-curtains' 19

C
calves, whale 24–25,
   27
carnivores 13
common dolphin 10–11

D
diving 13, 21
dolphins 6–7
  babies 24
  body parts 14–15
  bow-riding 21
  brains 11
  breathing 6, 12, 27
  catching fish 16
  keeping warm 15
  leaping 6, 26
  'melon' 17
  migration 23
  saving people 11
  schools 10
  size 6
  sleep 27
  squeaking 11, 17
  stranding 29
  swimming 11, 21
  teeth 7
  tricks 11, 21
dusky dolphin 26

E
echoes 11
Elizabeth I, Queen 23
eyes 9, 27

F, G
fat 15
fin whale 6
fins, dolphins 19
fish 16–17, 18
flippers 9, 15
food 13, 14, 16–17,
   18–19
grey whale 5, 24–25

H
heart 14
Hector's dolphin 19
humpback whale 8, 19,
   21, 23

hunting 16–17, 19,
   28–29

I, J, K
Indus River dolphin 9
Jonah 29
journeys 5, 23
killer whale 5, 20, 24
krill 13, 19

L, M
leaping, dolphins 6, 26
lungs 14
mammals 14–15, 18,
   24
migration 23
milk 24
minke whale 5
mouths 28

N, O
narwhal 22
orca 20

P
Pacific white-sided
   dolphin 21
Pakicetus 15
pilot whale 18
plankton 9
pods 17
porpoises 7
  body parts 14
  breathing 12
  migration 23

S
schools, dolphins 10–11
sharks 11
shellfish 9, 13
singing, whales 23
skeleton 14
skin 27
sleep 27
smell, sense of 7
sounds 11, 23
spectacled porpoise 7
speed 6
sperm whale 9, 12, 13,
   17, 18

squeaks 11, 17, 23
squid 17, 18
stomach 14
stranding 29
surfing 20
swimming 5, 6, 11, 16
swordfighting 22

T
taste, sense of 7
teeth
  dolphins 7
  killer whale 20
  narwhal 22
  porpoises 7
  whales 18
toothed whales 13, 17,
   18
touching 27
tricks 11, 21
tusk, narwhal 22, 23

W
weight, whales 5
whales
  babies 24–25
  baleen whales 13, 19
  barnacles on 8, 9
  'blows' 12, 13
  body parts 14
  brains 9
  breaching 8
  breathing 5, 12
  'bubble-curtains' 19
  diving 13, 21
  food 13, 14, 16–17,
    18–19
  journeys 5
  keeping warm 15
  living on land 15
  'melon' 17
  migration 23
  pods 17
  'singing' 23
  stranding 29
  toothed whales 13, 18
  tusks 22, 23
whale watching 27
whaling 28–29